# A Life Altar'd

Crystal Jones

ISBN: 978-1-7326765-0-3

ISBN-13:978-1732676503

# DEDICATION

*In loving memory of my Granny.*

*Laverne Hamilton thank you for your unconditional love and unending encouragement.*

# CONTENTS

# FORWARD

As the adage goes, I can honestly say that I don't look like what I've been through. "But by the grace of God I am what I am: and his grace which was bestowed upon me was not in vain…" (1 Corinthians 15:10). I am Mom to two wonderful sons and one beautiful daughter in law and Mama Crystal to two amazing step daughters and two adorable grandchildren. My family has been formed, molded, and knit together by the hand of God.

I wasn't the only casualty of the situations that shaped me. I have shared a couple of stories that are easiest to tell, and I have given the impossible ones to deal with to the Lord. I have made every attempt to be as vague as possible about certain details to protect others involved in this testimony.

I want to thank the Lord for the gift of writing this book. I would also like to express heartfelt gratitude towards my family and friends who are my support and inspiration in every season of life. My incredible and loving husband is the answer to every prayer that I never knew to pray, and I could not have done this without his reassurance.

Any encouragement or truth you can glean from the following pages can be directly attributed to the Lord Jesus Christ as there have been many prayers prayed that this book would find its way into the hands of someone who needs to hear how the One true and living God can alter a life set for destruction.

# 1 CHILDHOOD

*"Before I formed thee in the belly I knew thee; and before thou camest forth out of the womb I sanctified thee…" (Jeremiah 1:5)*

The following account of my life's story is an attempt to convey meaning and purpose found from the tragedy and triumph that I have known. The Hebrew root word for altar is lifted up. I am now living a lifted up life thanks to the Lord Jesus Christ who saved me from myself.

Growing up God wasn't relevant in my life. Though at first, I never knew the Lord, it is certain that he knew me. I can remember at some point going to Bible study at Grace Baptist church near our house and participating in AWANAS, but God never really resonated with me. The time spent there was more of a distraction to the harsh realities of my everyday life. Now, however, I can boldly proclaim that his blessings and mercies are without repentance, and there is no measuring of his love and grace. He saved me for a purpose. His peace truly surpasses our human ability to understand. He is an awesome God, and Jesus is his name. "Jesus saith unto him, I am the way, the truth, and the life: no man cometh unto the Father, but by me." (John 14:6).

From the outside we appeared to be a typical lower middle-class family. There were times we participated in team sports, went on vacations, and for a few years spent many weekends at farm lands on both sides of the family. Underneath the visible, however, there was a much more sinister and sad existence that we seemed destined to endure. I grew up in a modest single level brick ranch style home just west of Atlanta. My Sister and I, children to a father we wouldn't meet until late in our teen years, were almost one year apart in age. My half-brother was six years my junior. The shining light and beacon of hope in my life was my Granny. She had the unrealistic ability to make it all better no matter what it was. There were no second-class citizens at Granny's house. The situation with my stepdad's family was the complete opposite. My brother was their flesh and blood, and they made no bones about letting my sister and I know that we were the step children. From a very early age, I felt I didn't measure up, and there was nothing I could do to change it.

As I child I loved to read. My favorite author from the time I was seven to about fifteen when I stopped reading, was Stephen King. This coupled with my childhood experiences no doubt aided my dark personality. I read novel after novel of these evil stories. One book was over two thousand pages, and I read it when I was nine. To punish me as a child, or get my attention, they would take away my books. I had always wanted to be a mortician. From the time I was young, I had an unusual fascination with death. The wicked world I found myself a part of in my teenage years was a direct result of the material my mind had been filled with as a child. "Treasures of wickedness profit nothing: but righteousness delivers from death." (Proverbs 10:2).

Now that I am older I can see so many possible reasons for the torture we endured at the hands of my stepdad. He was a veteran, and though I am not sure on the details, there was some sort of injury. Maybe, he suffered from undiagnosed PTSD, or maybe he had suffered at the hands of his father, or maybe he was just crazy. One thing is for certain, the spirit that controlled him and reigned in our home was not of the Lord. There was no peace there. We lived in fear, walked on egg shells, and spent most of our childhood thinking of ways to kill or get away from him.

We often thought of poisoning him but could never seem to work up the courage to go through with it. We couldn't understand why our Mom subjected herself or us to life with him. He came outside one afternoon to help us practice softball after much coercing from her about needing to be involved with the family. None of us were happy about the idea of spending time together, but somehow my mom thought it was what we needed. He was not a small man. He lined my sister and I up against the brick wall at the back of our house and began to hurl softballs at us. As the crying and protest grew louder, my mom came out to defend us but was informed that she asked for this. He was teaching us not to be so afraid of the ball. We could either catch it or learn to suffer the consequences. We begged her to leave or to let us leave, but our cries fell on deaf and defeated ears.

He enjoyed afflicting us mentally almost more than physically. He was very sadistic and calculated in his efforts to make us uncomfortable, fearful, and heartbroken. Once he told us for weeks that we were all going to enjoy a nice family vacation at the beach. He hyped us all up so much about the joyous time we would have and was extra nice to everyone. On the day we were to leave he had us all pack our things and load the car while he sat in his recliner pretending to get himself ready. He told us all to go get in the car while he grabbed a few more things and we would be off. After several minutes of waiting my mom got out to see what the holdup was. We could see them arguing from the living room window and dread started to set in. Visibly angry and with a tear stained face my mom came to the car to inform us that there would be no vacation and we should go inside. If ever three kids begged for her to leave him; we cried and pleaded for her to take us without him. As we came into the house defeated, angry, and confused he let us know that he would never go on vacation with us. We were filth to him. He made us empty the car and unpack everything that very day. He chuckled and enjoyed watching our misery from his recliner as we labored to clean up any reminder of a vacation that was never meant to be. Every time she did manage to leave, she always ended up going back.

All in all, it wasn't the most terrible childhood. We did have some good times sprinkled in with the bad. Granny and Papa Billy took our cousins and us on many wonderful adventures, and we even had some good times at my stepdad's family land in North Georgia. We rode horses, played on the side of the mountain, and had some great experiences going on wagon trail rides. My mom did what she could, despite her distress, to make us feel loved and happy as children. Our elementary school was less than a mile from our house. We would often go up to the school to play on the playground and enjoy some free time. One afternoon our mom went with us up to the school. She taught us how to build forts and pretend houses from the pine straw on the school yard. It was an enjoyable afternoon. We laughed and relished each other. We were transported to another world that day where there was no care in our lives other than the here and now.

My grandparents, aunts, and even a school teacher tried to intervene but to no avail until one year when I was about fifteen she had enough and left him for the final time. We were finally free, and a new reality began to exist. My Mom liberated from the torture and chaos her life had been for the past several years decided to live like there was no tomorrow. She began drinking, partying, and soon bringing home men that seemed closer to my age than hers. We lived in a small duplex only a few streets away from the house I'd lived in most of my life. The duplex next to ours was empty and my sister and I, also wild and free, used it mostly for a party pad. We had friends and boys over there all the time drinking and doing drugs. I started dabbling in a dark and sinister world in that small duplex hosting a few séances and other sadistic group activities. I got my first job around this time at a local fast food restaurant to help my Mom with the never-ending bills that piled up each month, and to have money to support my new-found habits. Not long after this, as the divorce proceedings ended, my Mom got the house we grew up in, and we found ourselves back on that gloomy street that had always meant disaster for our family. Several times in the years that followed, as life ran its course, both my sister and I would end up coming back to live with our mom in this house for short periods.

As my Mom sunk deeper into a crazy lifestyle, my sister and I at fifteen and sixteen, decided we were ready to live on our own. We rented a trailer from my step dad's aunt in the next town and moved in.

My Sister had for many years carved out her own way in life. I always envied her independence and what I perceived as her ability to rise above our situation and make it. My brother had gone to live with his Dad in North Georgia. He was a phenomenal football player and seemed to have a bright future. But, the more he came to visit my mom's house and started to party the more he began to fall. By the time he was in his early twenties, he had been in and out of jail a few times, and his drug addiction fueled his diagnoses of schizophrenia. Sadly, to this day, he is not in his right mind and needs a miracle from God.

My biological father's mom, Maw maw, always came to visit my sister and I on our birthdays and Christmas. Our mom would never allow us to go and stay with her no matter how much she begged. As teenagers, we finally went to visit Maw

maw's house and met our real Dad for the first time. The first night
we met him he took us to a party with his friends, and we all got
drunk and high. Thus, he seemed not much different than our mom
until years later when he cleaned up and has since been the best
Dad and Grandpa he knows how to be.

Now living on my own I started dabbling into
stronger drugs than the marijuana and alcohol we had all shared at
my mom's old duplex. Acid, meth, and cocaine soon fueled my
day. I attended every hard rock, metal, and alternative band concert
I could afford to get into and found myself buried in the world of
rock and roll. I would often bring drugs and alcohol to school
unable to make it through the day without them. Barely able to
maintain the facade of normalcy I made it out of high school by the
skin of my teeth. High school is mostly a blur to me now. In my
freshman and sophomore years I was still trying to maintain the
image of a normal person and was making good grades in mostly
AP classes, but by the time junior and senior years rolled around,
my party lifestyle had caught up with me, and I was on a downhill

slope that would last for the next few years. While living with my

sister in the trailer and working at Burger King, I met my first

husband and father to my two children. Ours was a volatile

relationship to say the least.

# 2 MY FIRST ENCOUNTER WITH JESUS

*"And it shall come to pass, that whosoever shall call on the name of the Lord shall be saved." (Acts 2:21)*

After graduation, my fiancé and I decided it would be a great idea to move to Florida with my dad. We were struggling to make ends meet and wanted a fresh start. Along with a mountain of unpaid bills, we also left most of our things in Georgia. Sadly, a quick move and leaving behind our very minuscule amounts of material possessions would become the norm for our lives over the next several years. I never lived in the same place for more than a year at a time until I was in my late thirties.

We did okay in Florida at first. With my dad's help, we were able to get a car and eventually an apartment. We were so young and immature. Neither of us realized that seasonal jobs end when tourist season is over. We soon found ourselves in the same situation we were in back at home. We had no money and couldn't pay rent. We lost our apartment and slept in the Mustang for a while until we lost that. Our old neighbors dropped us off at the local bus terminal where we camped out with many of the other homeless people in the city. We would often walk for miles around the town to look for work. Sometimes he was able to get work at the day labor facility. One afternoon we talked a nearby hotel owner into letting us do a few odd chores for her. She paid us in cash at the end of the day. While walking back to the bus terminal, we stopped at Burger King and bought the two for four-dollar Whopper special. I remember those being the best tasting Whoppers I had ever had. Two homeless teenagers crashing with friends, or sleeping at the bus station, we were lost and without hope. For me, this was a familiar position to be in, but it seemed to fuel an inner fire in my then fiancé that caused him to do something that totally took me by surprise. After searching in the phone book and making a call, we walked a few miles to a local church to seek help. We had never discussed religion before; I guess because I didn't have any and he wasn't practicing. I knew his family attended church, but I had never really thought much about it.

As we walked, he was telling me this was a Pentecostal church, which meant nothing to me, and that I would probably see some scary things when I got there. I didn't understand what he was saying but what choice did I have. It was almost dark when we approached the church. I could hear the music before I could really see the building. It was a small church, and as we walked in, there were people standing, clapping, crying, dancing, shouting. What in the world was wrong with these people? Not soon after we got there, the music ceased, and the preacher got up to speak. I didn't understand a word he said, but the people seemed to like it. After the service concluded the preacher asked people to come up to the altar for prayer, and I remember just closing my eyes and hoping no one would speak to me. This man then invited us to his home next door to discuss our situation. The house smelled so nice. There were two large recliners in the middle of the room and sofas against the wall. His wife bustled about getting drinks and snacks, and I thought she was a genuine and nice person. I just kept quiet because I was totally out of my element. The preacher couldn't let us stay with him or in the church because we weren't married but he had an old trailer toward the back of the property that was being hauled away in a few days, and he agreed to let us stay there until it was taken. He walked us back over to the church where he found a box of peanut butter granola bars to give us. The trailer had no electricity or running water, but I slept the best I had slept in weeks. When you sleep outside you must keep one eye open to make sure your protected but, in that trailer, with a belly full of granola bars, I felt safe and hopeful for the first time since we lost our apartment.

The days spent in the trailer went by too quickly. As we made our way back to the bus stop, I decided I couldn't take it anymore. I used the pay phone to make a collect call to my Granny and beg for the chance to return home. Sometime later I would hear a Bible story about a young man who left home and got in a bad way and soon realized that even the least person in his dad's house was better off than him; so, he returned home with the hope that his dad would let him live with the lowliest of the household. "And when he came to himself, he said, how many hired servants of my fathers have bread enough and to spare, and I perish with hunger! I will arise and go to my father, and will say unto him, Father, I have sinned against Heaven, and before thee, and I am no more worthy to be called thy son: make me as one of thy hired servants." (Luke 15:17-19).

On the way back to Atlanta on the Greyhound bus, I asked every question I could think of about the church, the preacher, and the religion I had just encountered. Acts Chapter 2 was the main point of reference I was given. We planned to start attending his families' church when we got home and live a different type of life. Within the first few months of our return to Georgia, we became regular members of the small congregation. I was soon baptized in Jesus name and came up out of the water speaking in unknown tongues. "Then Peter said unto them, repent, and be baptized every one of you in the name of Jesus Christ for the remission of sins, and ye shall receive the gift of the Holy Ghost." (Acts 2:38). I immediately fell in love with the religion. I wanted to learn everything I could. We both began working and volunteering anywhere they would let us. In December that year, we married and found out our first son was on the way. I was eighteen when he was born.

I have encountered many people over the years that find the Apostolic Pentecostal religion tedious and constraining. To me, it was a breath of fresh air. I loved the black and white of it. The Bible says it, and we believe and live it. I heard a preacher say once that God is more concerned with our holiness than he is with our happiness. "Wherefore gird up the loins of your mind, be sober, and hope to the end for the grace that is to be brought unto you at the revelation of Jesus Christ; as obedient children, not fashioning yourselves according to the former lusts in your ignorance: but as he which hath called you is holy, so be ye holy in all manner of conversation; because it is written, be ye holy; for I am holy." (1 Peter 1:13-16). Holiness was so different and refreshing compared to the chaos of my childhood. My family was not religious at all and had a hard time with the way I choose to dress and live. "In like manner also, that women adorn themselves in modest apparel, with shamefacedness and sobriety; not with broided hair, or gold, or pearls, or costly array." (I Timothy 2:9). They accused me of joining a cult and worried that I had been brain washed. Nonetheless, I could not look back.

I was determined to the best Christian, wife, and mother I could possibly be. I wanted so badly to have a ministry like the other ladies in the church. I spent time with them learning about prayer and being a witness. We had several all-night prayer meetings where I learned to pray and seek God. My sweet Maw maw, seeing that I had not been taught much about cooking as a child, came over to my house for several weeks teaching me how to cook. She was so patient with me. I would read later that the Bible admonishes the older women to teach the younger. "The aged women likewise, that they be in behavior as becometh holiness, not false accusers, not given to much wine, teachers of good things; that they may teach the young women to be sober, to love their husbands, to love their children, to be discreet, chaste, keepers at home, good, obedient to their own husbands, that the word of God be not blasphemed." (Titus 2:3-5). Later in life, as I become stepmom to a lovely teenage daughter, I tried to apply these same lessons to her and her friends.

A visiting evangelist preached that everyone in the body of Christ has a ministry. He proclaimed that we all have a specific work to do. He went on to say that God has gifted us all uniquely to fulfill a certain role in the church. "For as we have many members in one body, and all members have not the same office: so we, being many, are one body in Christ, and everyone members one of another." (Romans 12:4-5). I couldn't imagine what my giftings and callings were. I really struggled with where I fit in. The evangelist then charged us to find our purpose starting with prayer and seeking God for direction. Unable to sing or speak in public I decided that prayer could be my ministry. I loved the idea of working behind the scenes. One afternoon, after laying my baby down for a nap, I went into my room and got on my knees. It was difficult to focus. I tried to concentrate on going deep in prayer. I had never spoken in tongues outside the church, but I knew that intercessory prayer required a true visitation and working of the Spirit. "For he that speaketh in an unknown tongue speaketh not unto men, but unto God: for no man understandeth him; howbeit in the spirit he speaketh mysteries." (1 Corinthians 14:2). As ridiculous as it seemed, I continued to talk to God. I had to refocus and be mindful of my thoughts, but miraculously, the more I pressed, the more the Spirit began to flow. It was amazing. I was so happy in my new-found place in the body. I could and would pray. I had asked the Lord to teach me to pray and would soon discover the disciples had asked the very same thing of him. "After this manner therefore pray ye: Our Father which art in Heaven, hallowed be thy name. Thy kingdom come. Thy will be done in Earth, as it is in Heaven. Give us this day our daily bread. And forgive us our debts, as we forgive our debtors. And lead us not into temptation, but deliver us from evil: for thine is the kingdom, the power, and the glory, forever. Amen" (Matthew 6:9-13).

I busied myself with the work of the church and tried not to pay attention to my failing marriage and the stress of being a young mother. I was in love with the religion and prayer, but I neglected the word of God. This would prove catastrophic in the tumultuous years that followed. The only knowledge I had of the word came from services attended or conversations with church members. It never really occurred to me to pick up the Bible, the very book I professed to live my life by and read it for myself.

When our second son came along, there was no end to his struggle. It seemed the enemy had him marked for destruction before he even breathed his first breath. I know now that all we went through with him was due to the heavy anointing and calling on his life. I had a very difficult pregnancy and a planned C-section. The baby had an infection, and we were moved to the children's ward of the hospital where he received several injections a day in his tiny little body. He had colic and was an

extremely fussy baby. It was almost impossible to soothe him.

One afternoon he had been crying nonstop for

hours when I got a knock on the door. My next-door neighbor, an

elderly woman, yelled at me as soon as I opened the door. She

said, "Can't you shut that baby up?" I was furious and exhausted.

Obviously, if I could have made him stop crying, I would have

long ago. I lost it in that moment and slung the baby into her arms.

I slammed the door and yelled at her, "If you think you can do

better then go for it!" I took a deep breath and re-opened the door

to see this poor woman standing white faced, in total shock, with

my screaming baby in her clutches. I just glared out her and said

give me my baby and slammed the door in her face. Sadly, we

never spoke much to our neighbor after that.

When he was three months old, they

found that one side of his body was growing faster than the other

and we were sent over to the hospital for further testing. They were

already speculating that he would have a permanent limp or

possibly need to use braces to walk. As I waited in the lobby for my baby to be returned to me, an elderly woman was shuffling index cards in her hands and speaking quietly to herself. I must have looked as terrified as I felt because she came over to me and asked if I was all right. I informed her of the news I had just received, and she just smiled and told me not to worry. She asked me his name, and upon hearing it, her grin became even bigger. She asked if I knew about the story of Jacob in the Bible. She told me that he was a man marked from the womb, he walked with a limp, and he knew hardships, but it didn't stop God from working in and through him.

Every six months from that day until he was seventeen I had to take our son for abdominal ultrasounds because his condition was known to cause tumors that can be associated with a certain type of cancer. But, God was merciful, and he never got any. He had a notable difference in the length of his two legs as a baby. My fear and concern over him as a small child turned to joy in him as a young boy and teenager. He has a wonderful sense of humor. He loves and walks after the Lord with an integrity far beyond his years.

Some marvelous things that happened during our years at the church. I gave myself to intercessory prayer, to the ministry of the lost, and to the children's ministry. We saw our youngest son receive a physical miracle, and my stepdad and brother both came to a revival service and received the gift of the Holy Spirit with the evidence of speaking in tongues. "For with stammering lips and another tongue will he speak to this people." (Isaiah 28:11). These events helped me to decide to forgive and love my mom. I couldn't hold a grudge against her when I had seen God's forgiveness and love firsthand. There were so many other powerful encounters with the Lord that I can't possibly name or even remember them all.

Every time we entered the church doors, attended events, entertained, or fellowshipped with our church family the masks went on. Satan, the enemy of our souls, is a liar. If he can't get someone to deny their Christianity, he is happy to have them impersonate it. I have learned that is takes more than a love of religion to be a true Christian. One must have a relationship and a daily walk with Jesus to be able to make it.

The stresses of life and our inability to give ourselves wholly to the Lord were tearing down our resolve to make it as a family. Backsliding, or falling away from the Lord, is not something that happens to anyone overnight. Sometimes you see it happening but feel powerless to stop it because you don't want to give up the sin you have let enter your life. "Thine own wickedness shall correct thee, and thy backslidings shall reprove thee: know therefore and see that it is an evil thing and bitter, that thou hast forsaken the Lord thy God, and that my fear is not in thee, saith the Lord of hosts." (Jeremiah 2:19). Such was the case in my situation. Slowly, one compromise after another I found myself without a church, a religion, and seemingly a Lord; although, he was always there. After eight years of marriage and truly trying to make it work for our boys we decided to get a divorce.

One of my first actions after the divorce was to cut my hair. My hair had been uncut for the past eight years according to Biblical standards on holiness and other principles taught in 1 Corinthians chapter 11. It was a sign of rebellion and way to show the Lord that I was on my own. To this day it remains one of my deepest regrets because a woman's hair is given her for a covering. This covering is something I could have used in the dark years that were coming. "But if a woman have long hair, it is a glory to her: for her hair is given her for a covering." (1 Corinthians 11:15).

# 3 THE FALL

*"The highway of the upright is to depart from evil: he that keepeth his way preserveth his soul. Pride goeth before destruction, and a haughty spirit before a fall." (Proverbs 6:17-18)*

After being mostly a stay at home mom for the past eight years, I found it almost impossible to make ends meet as a single mother with two young boys. Without the constant help of my family, we wouldn't have eaten or had a place to sleep most of the time. I got a job at a local truck stop on the night shift so I could get my boys to school during the day. Before my divorce was even final, I had started dating a young man that also worked there.

My sister and I decided that the only way we could possibly get ahead in life was to go to college. So, we enrolled together. I was working full time, attending school full time, raising two boys, and fighting to survive while not having two pennies to rub together. It never occurred to me in all this time to call on the Lord I once loved so dearly. I felt that because I had walked away from him that I didn't deserve his help and I put any thought of him out of my mind. "For they that hated knowledge and did not choose the fear of the Lord: They would none of my counsel: they despised all my reproof. Therefore, shall they eat of the fruit of their own way, and be filled with their own devices." (Proverbs 1:29-31)

The young man I was dating had asked for my help with a personal situation he was having regarding his eligibility to live and work in the country. I had little regard for marriage at the time, so I agreed to his proposal on the condition that my family and especially my children could not find out. Barely out of my first marriage I entered my second one with eyes wide open and heart completely closed. We were able to keep up the facade of just dating for several months as he was busy with his work and family and I was more than busy with everything I was trying to do. When it came time for him to apply for an updated status, the charade had to end, and we had to start being and living as a married couple.

There are certain times in everyone's life; moments that you can look back on and say that was a definite crossroad. For me and my children, this was the beginning of the end. My boys were coping with the divorce and their dad's move to another state as best they could. I was absent most of the time working, at school, or studying. Even when I was there my mind usually wasn't. But, we lived with Granny, and she made it okay for them. She took time with them and loved them back to happiness and then I ripped them from her home and made them come live with a man they barely knew. I think the move was almost as hard on them as the divorce was. My new husband's family barely spoke English, and our marriage was a challenge to say the least. We tried to be cordial and accommodating to each other, but none of us were happy. My ex-husband and I had agreed that the boys would come stay with him and his new wife during summer breaks. I think these were the happiest times for all of us. I didn't have to deal with the disappointment and sadness of my boys every day, and they got to escape for a few months.

Not able to make it work living in the basement of his family's home I moved into an apartment about an hour away. We were still married but happily not living together any more. Once he got his situation cleared up, we decided that we didn't really want to be married and I found myself divorced for the second time before I was thirty. Life was difficult. I couldn't juggle work, school, and motherhood so I dropped out of college.

If I stayed busy, which wasn't difficult during the day, I could ignore the guilt and disgust I had for myself. But, when night fell, and the boys were sleeping I was left alone with myself, and that proved to be disastrous for me. I hated being alone because I didn't want to think or feel. I hated myself and could barely ignore the nagging feeling that I had given up too soon on the Lord. I tried so hard to block out any attempt He made to reach me. I started drinking and going out. It wasn't long before I went back to doing drugs to numb the pain.

For a while, I was able to maintain some semblance of normalcy for my kids' sake, but it didn't take long for the mask to come off. I developed a deep fear of being home alone. The fear was so great that many nights I would sleep in the living room because I was too afraid to lie down in another room. I was unable to sleep and stayed awake most of the night in terror. I would often put chairs and other barriers in front of our doors to relieve my fear. To keep from being alone, I started hanging out with random men. I would have friends and sometimes perfect strangers that I met online over to my apartment after the boys were fast asleep. The danger of what I was doing never crossed my mind. I just didn't want to be alone with me.

Most young girls dream of falling in love with prince charming and being whisked away to a perfect life after a perfect wedding day. That was never a dream of mine. Those weren't the stories I was reading as a child. Sadly, my first encounter with the opposite sex happened as a young teen during a party when I was totally wasted. I had tried to be a good wife to my first husband, but after that, I had no regard for my body or those I invited to use it. I would learn later the harsh consequences of immoral sins. "Flee fornication. Every sin that a man doeth is without the body; but he that committeth fornication sinneth against his own body." (1 Corinthians 6:18). Somewhere during all my indiscretions, I let a young man come and live with us. I barely knew him. Again, a choice that had dire consequences for me and the boys. At first, he was nice enough. He always had a ready supply of drugs and alcohol and liked to party. But, it wasn't long before his harmful nature began to show. One night, as he was choking me on the couch in the living room, I felt my breath leaving my body, and I looked toward my kids' bedroom doors questioning how much they were hearing and if they were going to find their mother dead the next morning. I wondered, as I was struggling to breath, what would happen to them. Would they live with Granny or their Dad? Would they ever forgive me or know how much I truly loved them? Then for seemingly no reason at all, he stopped choking me and got up and went to bed. We continued to live with him a few more months after that.

I went from one bad relationship to another usually landing us back at Granny's house in between them. The boys were growing up, and I was blind to what my lifestyle was doing to them. I couldn't see past my own grief to begin to deal with theirs. I was on self-destruct, and there seemed to be no coming back from it.

# 4 THE DARK YEARS

*"Then goeth he, and taketh with himself seven other spirits more wicked than himself, and they enter in and dwell there: and the last state of the man is worse than the first. Even so shall it be also unto this wicked generation." (Matthew 12:45)*

I have been asked over the years why women stay in abusive relationships. Ministering at the county jail years later we discussed this topic several times as I shared my testimony. Humans tend to be creatures of habit. Habits can be good or bad, but as people we tend to stick with what's familiar. I had been dealing with abusive men since childhood. It is a terrible situation to be in, but one I knew how to deal with. There

is a definite lack of self-esteem that paralyzes you into staying.

You feel that you somehow warranted the abuse or are unable by

reason of your own misfortune to escape it. Sometimes we think

our love can change the person who claims to love us. I'm not a

phycologist, so I can only speak to my situation and the reasons

given me by the abused women I have encountered over the years.

Over the next several years every relationship got worse and worse

until I had no desire to live.

Once I met a man online that wanted to hook up

with me very late at night. I called my cousin and asked her to

babysit telling her some lie or another. I woke my boys up and

dragged them to her house. I drove into Atlanta to meet this

stranger. We had a nice dinner, but when we went back to his

apartment things got out of hand. Confirming every person who

ever said don't talk to strangers; I really thought I wouldn't make it

out of there alive. When I finally did leave I cried all the way to

my cousins' house, and then proceeded to wipe my face, pick up my kids, and go home to get them off to school and get to work. After a few days I was right back out there meeting new strangers.

I had a lifetime of practice wearing the mask of everything is okay with me. The first time I was every cheated on by a man I loved was probably when I lost my hope in the opposite sex, and became jaded towards the very idea of relationships. I had received a call from a young lady he worked with who said he needed to tell me the truth. I remember so vividly walking up behind him at the kitchen sink, where he was washing dishes, and relaying the strange phone call to him. I could literally feel the exhale and change in his body and my heart broke. I thought I had to be misunderstanding the situation. There was no way that someone I loved and trusted, someone who knew my past, would hurt me like this. We had an engagement to attend later that evening, and after tears and many unanswered questions I was told to pull myself together, and get through our obligations for the night. With a broken heart and no hope in my future happiness the dark cloud of depression overcame me. I did put on my mask and pretend, but it was all darkness on the inside. A few days later a group of friends came over to visit me. I sat on the floor with my back leaning against the door as they stood on the outside knocking. I couldn't face them or anyone. I just sat there and listened to them knock and cried until they left. I sat on the floor for a long time after that unable to pull myself out of the darkness. From then on, I had no regard for the men I met. I didn't care if they were married or not, and most of the time I didn't care to even know their names.

I wasn't addicted to sex or men, but to my own self-loathing. People can become addicted to anything. So, I drank, did drugs, and dated random people all to destroy the person I hated the most, yet could never seem to get away from; me. Once, I met a man online who I conversed with for several months. The man was from Pakistan and was a Muslim. We spoke often of meeting one another and he even talked of marriage. He said he couldn't marry a Christian, and I assured him I wasn't one. Eventually, I moved onto to other men and left off conversing with him. But, I had denied the Lord publicly and would often think of this later in life. Another time I met a man online and he offered to send me money. I received a money order in the mail a few days later, and when I went to the post office, with my kids in tow, to cash it I got into big trouble. The post office workers had called the police who brought me to the police station for questioning. The man had sent me a post office money order that was fake. I had fallen prey to an internet scam. I felt like such an idiot. My boys kept asking the policemen if they were going to take me to jail. They did release me and told me not to speak with men I meet online anymore, and especially not to accept money from, or give money to any of them. "Wine is a mocker; strong drink is raging: and whosoever is deceived thereby is not wise." (Proverbs 20:1). Although I never stopped online dating, I did only speak to men from this country after that. I was obsessed with filling a void, that wasn't going to be filled with anything but God, no matter how hard I tried. I would learn later that the Bible talks about this very thing. "And ye are complete in him, which is the head of all principality and power." (Colossians 2:10).

I can only say about these years that I am so sorry for what my children had to go through. I can't take it back. If I could I would. They were so adorable and tolerant of me. They trusted me to love them and care for them, even though time and again I put them last. I had become my mother. I so vividly remember my sister and I talking about how we would never treat our kids the way we were treated. That we would never choose a man over them. Of course, I didn't see it that way. I loved them, but I didn't love myself enough to do what was best for any of us. My oldest son bore the brunt of my escapades. He was left to care for his younger brother many times. He was a child himself, but he truly became his brother's keeper and protector. He put himself in harm's way to shield his brother, and always picked up my slack around the house. These years really took a toll on him. God is so merciful though, and now he is a loving husband and a devoted father. I couldn't be prouder of the man he has become.

Years later, as I would visit the local jail and cry with the ladies I came to minister to about these situations, I would see one after another of them reach for the Lord in a desperate

attempt for forgiveness for some these very same sins. It doesn't

make it better or take away from the pain, but God is so gracious to

be able to use my mistakes to help someone else find hope in him.

I would find out years later that this is exactly how He operates.

"And they overcame him by the blood of the Lamb, and by the

word of their testimony; and they loved not their lives unto death."

(Revelations 12:11).


    I met my third husband during these dark years. I

knew he wasn't a good guy from the beginning, but I wasn't

exactly in the market for a good guy. My boys were on their annual

summer visit to their dad's house when we started dating. They

came back to find this man living in our home. We were always

struggling for money; mainly because I was the only one working,

and we liked to drink and smoke marijuana a lot. We had long,

loud, and scary fights in front of whoever had the misfortune of

being in the area. My boys spent many nights home alone while I

was out on the street corner with him. One night a storm came up and a tree fell through the roof of our apartment. My oldest son had to call me several times before I finally answered. He sounded so scared and desperate on the other end of the line. He recounted the story of the tree coming through and getting himself and his brother to safety. He made sure I knew the rain was still pouring in. When I finally did arrive home, I made him promise not to tell anyone they were home alone when it happened.

I maintained relationships with other men openly during the first few years of our relationship which led to intense battles. I didn't respect myself and I showed zero respect for him. Our house was filled with a constant haze of smoke, and flow of random people in an out at all hours of the day and night. It was a miserable place to be. My oldest son would lock his baby brother in their room when things got ugly to try and shelter him from what was happening. I know all too well exactly how they felt.

After one summer at their dads, my boys got home and asked me to come into their room, so we could talk. I remember it like it was yesterday. Another moment that forever altered our trajectory. I stood in front of these young men as they began to talk I couldn't believe how grown they looked. Where had my sweet baby boys gone? Had time really been going by this quickly? The oldest began to explain that while he visited his dad they had went to church. He loved how he felt there. He wanted to know more about the Lord, and knew that he couldn't do that living here with me. He loved me, they both did, but they felt it would be better if they moved up to their dads' house to stay so they could go to church. I felt as if he had just slapped me. What the world was this kid saying? Every drop of anger, resentment, self-loathing, and I don't even know what came over me. The Spirits that controlled me, sensing what was to come, came out with a fight. I cursed those poor sweet boys from head to toe. I called them everything under the sun, and cursed the days they were born. Bless their hearts. They never faltered. With tears streaming, and physically shaking, they stood their ground and took my berating like men. I left them standing there for fear of what I might do considering how I was feeling. I went into my room and slammed the door. Their Dad also came to over to inform me that he knew what was going on in the home, and I could either cooperate with the boys request, or he would call and report me to the proper authorities. That night as I lay down to sleep I heard the voice of God. I knew it was Him even though I hadn't heard his voice in close to ten years. Praise him, as I struggle to write this through the tears all I can say is he intervened on their behalf. "And God heard the voice of the lad; and the angel of God called to Hagar out of heaven, and said unto her, What aileth thee, Hagar? Fear not; for God hath heard the voice of the lad where he is." (Genesis 21:17). He said, "What are you doing? You know you must let them go. They can't stay here. Do you really want this for them?" I cried for them for the first time. I went back into their room where they had retired to their beds and just simply said you can go.

Plans were made, and they were to leave at the end of summer. After spending a week in Florida, being spoiled and loved on by my Dad and Maw maw, the youngest one said on the drive home that he could just stay and let his brother go so I wouldn't be alone. I knew he was just getting a little scared to leave everything he had ever known. I told him no, and that he needed to go. I knew he couldn't stay because it would destroy him.

With the boys gone there was no end to the fighting and chaos in my home. Things went from bad to worse very quickly. I was working on a job with my sister at the time, and I know her influence with the boss is the only reason I was able to stay employed. He had mentioned a few times about my attendance and appearance. I would come straight from the club to work usually still drunk or high. My work was being affected by my lifestyle. There seemed to be no end to my boyfriends' craziness. He would often call and threaten me, my sister, and other co-workers. I literally wished to die every day. I saw no reason to continue. I felt that my boys were finally safe, and I really had no reason to exist other than to be miserable, and someone's punching bag.

I became consumed with the idea of how I would meet my end. I didn't want to overdose on drugs feeling it was to cliché because of my family's history with drug addiction. While I was busy trying to find ways to leave this world, my boys had found a new lease on life. They were both baptized in Jesus name and filled with the Holy Spirit. God began to work in their lives and give them both callings for service. Miraculously, they forgave me for all the wrongs I had done to them, and started to pray for me. I had never asked for their forgiveness or prayers, but they gave it nonetheless. They called me countless times to ask me to go to church. I don't even know if they knew that I had done the religion thing before and failed at it. I certainly had no intention of going down that road again. No, my only option was suicide. "The way of peace they know not; and there is no judgement in their goings: they have made them crooked paths: whosoever goeth therein shall not know peace. Therefore, is judgement far from us, neither doth justice overtake us: we wait for light, but behold obscurity; for brightness, but we walk in darkness." (Isaiah 59:8-9).

# 5 THE LIGHT AT THE END OF THE TUNNEL

*"O remember not against us former iniquities: let thy*

*tender mercies speedily prevent us: for we are brought very low. Help us, O God*

*of our salvation, for the glory of thy name: and deliver us, and purge away our*

*sins, for thy name's sake." (Psalms 79:8-9)*

I had decided that I could make my boyfriend, who threatened to kill me often, do the deed for me. I tried everything I could think of to antagonize and goad him. I made a horrific situation even worse. No matter how much I tried he wasn't going to kill me. I decided then that I would drive my car down the highway and ram it into the median. It would be an accident, and no one would be the wiser. After one bad argument I got my speed up, and decided today was the day. Moments before I was to jerk the wheel to the left I caught a glimpse of my funeral. My boys and Granny were there. They were crying and saying it was their fault. The boys were saying if they wouldn't have left it wouldn't have happened. Granny was trying to figure what more she could have done to love me back to sanity. What? I didn't want them to feel these things. My decisions weren't about them. I decided to wait until I had a little more time to think.

The boys were relentless. They were always asking me to go to church. I finally conceded, and went a few times to the church up the street that they had chosen. Remarkably, a few years before that the baby boy had come home from school begging to join Boy Scouts. Everyone was doing it and he just had to. I didn't have time or the desire to drive far, so I had taken both to Boy Scouts at this very church for several months. They had both made friends and even attended a few services and outings. I had totally forgotten about it until I drove into the parking lot. Honestly, the first few trips I made to the church were a blur. I went a few times still drunk and high from the night before. I was

defeated, disgusted, and determined to leave this world. I knew

there was nothing for me at the church. I was happy that the boys

had their new life, and thought it was sweet of them to want me to

be included in it, but this wasn't the answer for me. However, I

kept coming to church because it seemed to be the only topic my

kids wanted to discuss with me.


All my life I have suffered with depression and

self-esteem issues. I have never been a skinny girl. I have always

struggled with my weight, and the deep depressions I would sink

into because of my inability to deal with my own life situations,

didn't help. Depression, for me, is like a dark cloud that I can see

approaching. It is ominous. Knowing it is coming, but being

powerless to stop it, I have always just let it overtake me. During

times of depression I let food be my comfort; unable to find little

comfort in anything else in my life it was my one source of peace.

From the time I was young, my step dad went to extreme lengths to

make me feel less than and inadequate. The years of abuse I

subjected myself to at the hands of random men only added to my already miniscule sense of self-worth. These issues coupled with the weight I seemed to always be putting on were just fuel for the fire. Is it any wonder, that as I attended a church where I was always hearing about the love and forgiveness of God, that I was unable to make the connection that these were offerings being made to me? No, I couldn't and wouldn't entertain the thought that the God I had once chosen to walk away from would want me back. Not after the things I had allowed in my life in the recent years. The first time I came to the Lord I had felt as if my life situations were done to me, and that I was just a victim of my circumstances. But, this time I had brought about my own destruction. Years later I would own the fact that many of the situations I found myself in, even as a young teenager, were products of my own sinful nature and habits. Yes, some things were out of my control, but not everything. I would come to know that God had always been there. However, in this moment, I just could not except that I could come back to the Lord. Honestly, I was angry with Him. Angry at the Lord who found me and then let me go. I felt that if He had really loved and wanted to save me He would have fought harder to keep me. I know now that God doesn't operate like that. He is just and merciful, yes, but He is also a gentleman, and has given humans the right and ability to choose Him or not. "But every man is tempted, when he is drawn away of his own lust, and enticed." (James 1:14).

My mission to put myself out of my own misery was on the forefront of my mind every day. I hated myself and my life. After some intense days at home I had decided that the boys and Granny, in time, would find their own peace with my decision, and I could no longer put it off. I had to end it and soon. I went to church one last Sunday to make the boys happy, or so I thought. I had determined that morning that today would be the day. I walked in and took my usual position near the back of the sanctuary, to make a speedy escape, during the altar call. I don't remember the message that was preached or any of the songs that were sung; I just know that when I got up to leave the Lord arrested me. Just as He had done a few years earlier when the boys asked me to let them go; He spoke to me in an almost audible voice. It was so loud and clear that I looked around to see if anyone else had heard it. He said, "Choose me or die." At first, I just scoffed and said I have already chosen to die. Choose me or die echoed in my mind. I couldn't move. He clearly wanted a decision before I took one step towards the door. I knew that if He allowed me to leave I would go straight to the highway and into the median. I was determined to see it through today. Choose me or die; I began to shake and look around. I started to plead with Him, "Lord, look at these people. They are so perfect. They don't look like me. I don't talk them. They have their perfect little families and perfect hair and clothes. These women are beautiful. What could I possibly have to do with them. They wouldn't want me around. I have nothing to give here. I can't." He simply said, "Choose me or die." I couldn't stop the tears or the shaking. I was so lost and didn't really want to be found. I didn't want to try Him again and fail. I couldn't take another disappointment like that in myself or Him. The same words echoed over and over. I felt as if I was the only person in the world, even though I was in a building with hundreds of people.

I'm not sure exactly what happened next. My subsequent thought was walking to my car and telling the Lord that I can't have this and that. I didn't want to feel this way and go home to the anarchy that was my life. If he was going to be real with, and me with him, then it had to one hundred percent and never looking back. For that, I knew I needed his divine intervention. The Bible gives us a word of encouragement for just such times. "Be strong and of a good courage, fear not, nor be afraid of them: for the Lord thy God, he it is that doth go with thee; he will not fail thee, nor forsake thee." (Deuteronomy 31:6). I didn't make it a mile up the street before being overtaken by the Spirit again. I pulled over crying and speaking in tongues. He was washing and preparing me. I picked up the phone and dialed my boys. For the first time in their lives I apologized to them for what I had put them through. I begged for the forgiveness they had already given me. I spoke to both boys, and we were all crying and speaking in tongues. I promised them that I would never go back to being what I was when I walked into the church that morning, and by the grace of God I haven't.

As I pulled up to my apartment I was scared that I couldn't do it. Self-doubt and fear were trying to stop me from doing what I knew needed to be done. I prayed for strength, climbed the stairs and got to work. The house was littered with alcohol and drug paraphernalia that I just walked past and ignored. I went into my room and gathered up some important documents and few clothes and walked back down to my car. I had to get out. I couldn't stay there. Almost everything in the place was mine. The apartment and utilities were all in my name because I was the only one working and paying for it, but I couldn't stay. By the grace of God my boyfriend wasn't home. There would be no fighting that day. I left and just drove around for hours. I parked a few times unable to control the crying and prayer that went on. I had so much buried deep within that I just gave it all to Jesus. I was in the car for a few days before I decided that I needed to go to Granny's to shower and plan. My poor, dear Granny had been through so much with her kids and grandkids over the years. She was heartbroken that the boys had moved away, even though she knew they had too. I walked in and asked to use the shower. She was leery of my motives, and rightfully so. When I got out of the shower I sat to have some food with her. She immediately noticed and commented that I looked different. I told her that I had been to church, and realized that I could no longer live the way I had been for the past few years. I knew I had to change. I told her I left my apartment. She thought about it for bit and offered to let me stay there if there was no indication I was going back to my old lifestyle. She threatened to put me out at the first sign of trouble. I was thankful and honestly, I had no faith in myself that I could do it, but with the help of the Lord I was going to try. I went to church every time the doors were open. I attended every class they offered. I went to work and home to Granny's. I cut off every contact from my old life. I had to isolate myself completely from that world if I really wanted to make this work.

This time I was determined to know the Lord. I spent hours reading and studying the Bible. I wanted to know it, and Him for myself. I was seeking a relationship not a religion. I had to make sure that I knew the Lord enough to fight and overcome my inner demons. My passion for reading had returned, and this time I wasn't going to read anything that would destroy my soul, or feed my flesh. I began trying to eat right and walking for miles a day to get control of my body. It made me feel wonderful.

Then for some reason, in a moment of weakness, I opened a door that almost caused me to lose myself and this relationship with the Lord again. I accepted a phone call from my old boyfriend. He noticed the change in me and was struggling in life. After I left he had to find a place to live and a way to support himself. He said he missed me, but I know now that was not the case. He said everything I had ever wanted and needed him to say. I began to listen to the subtle enticements of the enemy of my soul being spoken through this man's voice. I told myself what a glorious testimony it would be if we could proclaim that the Lord had rescued us both from the pits of hell and turned our lives around. He started coming to church with me, and was baptized in Jesus name. He never received the Holy Spirit, but the Bible says if you are baptized in the name the gift of the Spirit is yours; and I do pray that one day he will come to know the Lord in His fullness that his soul might be saved. I told him that we could not live together again unless we were married. I was determined to live a new life. We attended marriage counseling at the church and were soon married. We moved in with my sister and her kids. Thus, he became husband number three.

All was well for a couple of months. He did try to make it work. I saw him many times reading his Bible and turning down invitations to hang out on the old street corner. We visited the boys often and they were pleased with the changes that were taking place in both of our lives. On one trip he was driving, and put in a music CD to listen to. The music had terrible lyrics full of cursing and sexual innuendo. I had liked these songs before, but the spirit in me was cringing at hearing them now. I told him how I felt and was surprised when he became enraged. He took the CD and threw it out the window. He stated that just because your religious shouldn't mean you can't enjoy life. I countered with the fact that there was nothing good or enjoyable about that music. A little while later when we stopped for gas and he wanted money to buy a lottery ticket. I told him that we shouldn't play the lottery. Christians shouldn't gamble or waste money on such frivolous things. Again, he became enraged stating that religion was like chains to him. I couldn't disagree more. To me it was the breaking of chains and strongholds. This was my first indication of where his heart truly lied. He was so frustrated that he stayed in the hotel room while I went to the church to see my youngest son get baptized.

As we moved into our own home I was racked with how to proceed with my boys. I had prayed so often that the Lord would return them to me. I knew they were happy and flourishing, but I was saved now and wanted so badly to be their mom again. After many months I stopped praying to get them back, and started asking the Lord to make a way for me to be near them. It was coming close to the time for my oldest son to graduate high school and he had plans to attend Bible college. I decided that

I needed to go back to college to finish my degree, so I could afford to move close to them, and get a good job to help finish raising them. Oh, what a tangled web we weave when we try to help God with the plans He has for our lives, instead of trusting in His ways and processes. I took early retirement from my job and started back to school the next semester. Busy with school, my new internship, and activities at church I was easily able to avoid all the signs that my new husband was struggling with his newfound faith, and was slipping back into his old lifestyle and habits.

My Granny's health was declining around this time. She had been diagnosed with MS, and after several falls, and using a walker for a while, had been confined to a wheelchair. I moved back home with her for what I said was to help take care of her, but I was really struggling financially, and the move helped me probably more than it did her. Moving back to Granny's proved to be disastrous for my husband. We were way too close to the old neighborhood and the unending call he felt for his old life. I found myself in a very undesirable situation. He was married to the

streets and I just wanted to be married to the Lord. I didn't know

what to do. My old self-loathing returned. I told myself that I knew

better than to think I could live this life. Here I was professing to

know and love the Lord, and yet was getting close to a possible

third failed marriage. Who did I really think I was? I knew the

Bible spoke against divorce and I also knew that I couldn't live

like I had before with him. The fighting had started getting worse

and more often. Only now, instead of my kids being in the middle

of it, my poor Granny had to endure it all.

My sister really helped me when I was at my

wits end. Her and my niece had started visiting the church. They

were both baptized and filled with the Holy Spirit. She forced her

way, with me in tow, to the family pastor of the church, and let

him know I really needed help with a situation. He was so gracious

and kind. I felt like the biggest joke. I promptly told him that I

didn't really need help because I already knew what he would say,

so there was no point in discussing it. This he found very

frustrating, and insisted that I meet with him to discuss what I thought might be the answers he would give me. I was beyond nervous when I sat in the office. At first I tried to be very vague, but before I could help it I was spilling out the gory details of my marriage. To my surprise he let me know that God loved me. The Lord had no intention of me being someone's doormat. There were certain roles that husbands and wives are assigned to in the Bible. He pointed out scriptures and gave me advice to follow. I tried to do it my way at first, but eventually had to follow his suggestions when nothing else seemed to work. I told my then husband that I had decided to follow Jesus and he could either follow Him or not, but I would not live or be a party to a lifestyle that is contrary to the teachings of the Bible. He chose to leave.

I never stopped coming to church, but I sat amid the congregation feeling like a total failure. I had worked so hard to overcome my past only to let myself get tangled right back up in a bad situation. I am so thankful that during this time the Lord helped me stick close to him so that I wouldn't be lost again. Now more determined than ever, I did what I knew to do which was dive into the word of God, throw myself into service for the church, and stay within the confines and safety of Granny's house until I could face the world without being tempted by it. "Wherefore let him that thinketh he standeth take heed lest he fall. There hath no temptation taken you, but such as is common to man: but God is faithful, who will not suffer you to be tempted above that ye are able; but will with the temptation also make a way to escape, that ye may be able to bear it." (1 Corinthians 10:12-13).

It was during this time that I started visiting our jail ministry. One night one of the leaders suggested that I might be a good person to teach and minister to the ladies. This terrified me, and I never returned to visit until years later. Putting myself and my story out for everyone to see was not on my to do list. I also did not want any part of standing in front of anyone to speak, even if I was talking about the Lord.

Also, during this time, the Lord answered my prayers in a most remarkable way. Out of nowhere my kids' dad called to tell me they were moving back to Georgia. What the world? Just like that they were coming back. I would learn later of the principles of sowing and reaping from the Bible. God can completely change our lives, but we must still pay for the sins we commit. "They that sow in tears shall reap in joy." (Psalms 126:5). We reap what we sow. In my life, as I began to sow good seeds of love, patience, and forgiveness I began to reap good rewards, however, I still had to pay for all the years I had sown bad seed. Part of that payment for me was all the years spent away from my children. I can never get those years back. "Even as I have seen, they that plow iniquity, and sow wickedness, reap the same." (Job 4:8). I didn't know what to expect, but I was so grateful that they would be close, and I would get to see them often. I knew that I could not falter. There was no way I was going to disappoint those boys again. They had left as children and were coming back as young men. The whole dynamic of our family was changed as we were all striving to live Christian lives.

As my relationship with Lord grew deeper any old resentments I had toward people in my life disappeared. The Lord has a way of making forgiveness work. "But if ye forgive not men their trespasses, neither will your Father forgive your trespasses." (Matthew 6:15). The boys, their dad, his family, and I had a good relationship. When I visited the boys, before they moved back, we often ate and fellowshipped together. We had all been forgiven things by the Lord and had taken that forgiveness and turned it into a mutual respect. We put our focus on the boys and making the situation work for them. So often people ask how our families can get along so well, and all I can say is that God is good.

My kids' stepmom never looked down her nose at me. She always treated me with respect and care as their mother. She knew the gory details of my situation when the boys came to live with them, but she never judged me. She always made me feel welcome when I came to visit and included me on any major decisions where the boys were concerned. She treated the boys as hers, and mine, from day one. Years later when I became a stepmother to two amazing girls I tried to treat their mothers as I had been treated. Come to find out that is the Bible way! "And as ye would that men should do to you, do ye also to them likewise." (Luke 6:31).

# 6 THE STANDING YEARS

*"Stand therefore, having your loins girt about with truth,*

*and having on the breastplate of righteousness;" (Ephesians 6:14)*

I heard a remarkable sermon preached at our district conference one year. The minister discussed the different seasons in life, and our concurrent actions during those times of walking, standing, and sitting. "Blessed is the man that walketh not in the counsel of the ungodly, nor standeth in the way of sinners, nor sitteth in the seat of the scornful. But his delight is in the law of the Lord; and in his law doth he meditate day and night. And he shall be like a tree planted by the rivers of water, that bringeth forth his fruit in his season; his leaf also shall not wither; and whatsoever he doeth shall prosper." (Psalms 1:1-3). It was so true to life that I will never forget it. As I struggle with the ever-changing seasons we, as Christians, go through I try to hold onto the truths in that message.

I was complete, for the first time in my life, in Him. I was happy. I had started making a few friends at the church. I had also started working with the homeless ministry and evangelizing in the streets with a few friends on the weekends. I was learning so much about myself and the Lord. I was being stretched and shaped into an actual Christian lady. Almost without my knowledge the callousness of my former life was falling from me. Instead of a hard woman with a cheeky personality I was becoming a helpful and caring person. I cared for people other than myself and those of my inner circle. I no longer felt cynicism toward the world. God is miraculous in this way. When we walk with him we are changed from the inside out. True relationship with him will change you. "Therefore, if any man be in Christ, he is a new creature: old things are passed away; behold, all things are become new." (2 Corinthians 5:17).

The Bible gives us a beautiful example of what a woman should be. We call her the Proverbs 31 woman. Mirroring her example was my goal. "She openeth her mouth with wisdom; and in her tongue is the law of kindness. She looketh well to the ways of her household, and eateth not the bread of idleness." (Proverbs 31:26-27). I was given the opportunity to share my testimony at the lady's prayer group at church, the homeless ministry, and at the P7 Bible club my son was hosting at his high school. I couldn't believe how the Lord was changing me from the inside out.

Both boys had come to stay with me not long after the move. As my oldest son prepared to head off to Bible college I had some tough decision to make. I knew that I could not afford a private college and maintain our household with my current salary. Now in my senior year of college, and working in the field of accounting as a staff accountant; I had no choice but to make some major changes. There was no way I was going to sacrifice my son's dream of going to the college of his choice because of the poor decisions I had made in my own life. I would gladly give up anything to make sure my children could accomplish their goals in life. I left college one semester shy of graduating, and left the world of accounting to enter the world of staffing. I also took a second job to supplement my income. Later, I would realize this was exactly where God wanted me to be. It is no wonder he doesn't let us know the plans he has for us because we would without a doubt try to change his mind; like we could know what would be best. "For I know the thoughts that I think toward you, saith the Lord, thoughts of peace, and not of evil, to give you an expected end." (Jeremiah 29:11).

After my oldest son returned early from Bible school we moved into a small house a few streets over from Granny's. My son, now an adult, chose to go a different path. It was a heartbreaking decision for me, and extremely difficult for his little brother. I wrote the following poem a few years later. It is an

expression of my love and concern for him and his choices at the

time. I am including it in hopes that it will help someone who has a

family member that has chosen to walk away from God. Perhaps,

for you as it is to me, this poem can be the beginning of a prayer

for their safety, peace, and restoration with the Lord.

*"For My Son Who is Struggling"*

*If I could take back every hateful word*

*Every time I left you alone*

*Every time I choose me over you*

*I would, but I can't*

*If I could take your struggles, your fears, your pain*

*And make them mine*

*I would, but I can't*

*If I could help you to see how the Lord saved me*

*How He pulled me up from the depths*

*Oh, that my victory could be your victory*

*But, it can't*

*If I could relate to your struggles*

*I would, but I can't*

*If I could show you my childhood filled with abuse,
sadness, fear, and disappointment*

*If living through my past would save you the trouble of
choosing the wrong road*

*I would let you live it*

*But, I can't*

*If you could stand in my shoes and listen to your child tell
you that he must move away*

*To find peace and know the Lord*

*If you could feel my heart breaking, not because you were
wrong*

*But, because I knew you were right*

*If you could feel that pain*

*Oh, if it would change your direction*

*But, it won't*

*If you could see me talking to you on the phone*

*Crying, listening to how great you are doing, and how
awesome Church is*

*If you only knew how many times I thought the world would
be so much better off without me in it*

*If that would make you wake up*

*But, it won't*

*If you could know how proud I was to see you preach, to
hear you quote scripture*

*To listen to you speak in tongues*

*If my joy could make your heart sing*

*But, it can't*

*If you could have been in church that day*

*If you could have heard Him tell me that I had to choose*

*If my decision could save both our souls*

*But, it can't*

*If I could only understand what would make you give up
your dreams, your calling, your friends, your college, your faith*

*But, I can't*

*If I could find a way to tell you to turn around and run to
Him*

*But, I can't*

*If you would listen to the Holy Ghost within you*

*Even common sense would say that you have already lost
more than you've gained on this road*

*If you would only turn around*

*If you could see how sad it makes me to see you struggle*

*I know my past is under the blood, but with every victory
you give the devil*

*I can't help but feel guilty*

*If I could have been a better, a true Christian, and Mom*

*Oh, that I could help to save your soul*

*But, I can't*

*If you only knew that such a handsome, intelligent, witty,
talented, and awesome guy*

*Doesn't have to just exist in this life*

*Settling for second best isn't in your nature*

*He has saved you, created you, and destined you for greatness*

*If you would only let Him lead the way*

*But, you won't*

*When I hear you say you know both roads and you are choosing this one*

*If only you could understand that I too chose that road, and that is the reason your life was so hard*

*If my bad choices could be a lesson to you*

*But, they can't*

*If I could get you into Heaven*

*I would*

*But, I can't*

*If He hadn't loved us so much*

*He would have left us there on Cemetery Street dying in sin*

*But, He didn't*

*If you only knew all the prayers that touch His throne for you*

*But, you can't*

*You won't, I can't*

*But, He can, and I know that He will*

*And I won't stop praying until He does*

During an all-night prayer meeting at a friends' house I felt the Lord speaking to me about the way I looked. I also saw a vision for the first time in my life. The image was quick and fleeting, but I saw it nonetheless. I saw myself standing next to a man; the man was clearly my husband although I was not, nor had any intention of becoming, married. We were preaching and witnessing to a crowd of people. The people were praying and crying out to the Lord. The me that I saw was not the same me I was that day. I was much thinner. I tried not to read too much into it. When I went home the boys and I were having a conversation about weight. They were weighing each other and after much protest I agreed to step on the scale. I was at my highest weight of three hundred and twenty pounds. We discussed making some major changes. I knew this coupled with the vision I had were a sign of changes that needed to be made. I was determined to become the woman I had seen in that vision. "What? Know ye not that your body is the temple of the Holy Ghost which is in you, which ye have of God, and ye are not your own?" (1 Corinthians 6:19). I started eating healthy and walking every day. After a few months my oldest son encouraged me to run. I thought he was being ridiculous. There was no way I could run; I could barely walk. But, I started jogging very slowly for a few steps during my daily walks, and eventually was jogging for half of the five miles I was doing per day. I had been invited to visit Peru with a friend from church in a few months' time, and was making that my number one stop to my current weight loss goal. Within eight months I had lost an amazing eighty pounds. I had never felt better in my adult life. From that time until now I must be mindful of what I eat, and be diligent about exercise. My weight fluctuates, but I remain determined not to get back to where I once was. With my son now home from school I was able to drop the second job and focus more time on working out and ministry.

Turns out my new position as a recruiter helped in my ministry efforts. The position allowed me the opportunity to help people that we met in the street ministry with getting employment. I was also able to bless a few in our church with much needed work. My co-workers were always curious about my Christian walk. One afternoon they were sharing some food and asked if I wanted to join them. I declined, but they refused to accept this without a truthful explanation as to why. I explained to them that this day happened to be my fast day. They were shocked. They couldn't believe that people fasted. Most of them were a lot younger than me, and some had heard of fasting, but thought it was an ancient practice. I told them that fasting, prayer, my appearance, and the many other ways they saw me live my life were all a part of being a Christian. "And be not conformed to this world: but be ye transformed by the renewing of your mind, that ye may prove what is that good, and acceptable, and perfect, will of God."

(Romans 12:2). We had a long discussion that day about religion and relationship with the Lord. They were also very generous to the causes I championed. They gave often to the ministries I worked in, and would for many years to come.

I started back to jail ministry, as well. If I could share my testimony with total strangers on the street I could surely do it for the ladies I would encounter. In one session a young lady asked me, "How did you do it, like the getting off drugs, I know you say it, but how did you do it?" To this I responded that it is only possible by taking one day at a time. There were days that I wanted a drink, or to get high, and there were other days that I wanted to call a male friend because I felt lonely. First, if you haven't, you must be saved in the only way the Lord has told us how to be in the Bible. We must repent for our sins and be baptized in Jesus name for the remission of those sins. His name is the only name given whereby we must be saved. And then, the Bible promises that we will receive the gift of the Holy Spirit. The evidence of having received the Holy Spirit is speaking in tongues. This is the Bible way. Without His spirit living and working in me

I would still be in the streets or dead. I certainly wouldn't have had

the power to live an overcoming life. I knew that if I went back

even one time I would be lost again. I started by waking up every

day and deciding to live on purpose. Before my feet hit the floor, I

would pray to the Lord for direction and covering. I would ask that

He take away unclean desires from me and keep my heart and

mind focused on him. I would then read the Bible. When the urges

hit, I would pray either out loud or to myself, depending on where

I was. I tried to stay as busy as possible by going to church

whenever there was service, and volunteering for anything I could.

The more I focused on doing for others the less I was worried

about pleasing my own selfish desires. The first year was hard, the

second year was easier, and after that it got easier and easier. It

takes determination, willingness to put in the work, and a faith in

God to help you along the way. Being a Christian doesn't mean

you won't struggle with things. We are human and live in a sinful

world. There is an enemy of our souls seeking to destroy and

devour whomever he can. The battles become different the longer

you know and walk with the Lord. As a former addict I know that I have to be more conscious than the average person about what I give my time and attention too.

Nowadays, my overcoming struggle would be with weight loss. Ugh, that is a difficult battle. You know what you should and shouldn't do, but when the desire hits you feel almost powerless to stop it, unless you are otherwise motivated. If you have determined to change it becomes easier to resist the urge to cheat until one day you don't even desire bad foods anymore.

I still fight battles but now they look different than the addictions of the past. I like everything in its place. I do the same things the same way every day, and can get very agitated when anything gets out of order. I think the chaos and inability to control anything in my life before makes me desire to be overly controlling now. But, God is working on me with this every day. He has given me a wonderful husband and amazing children to help remind me that I am not in control, and everything doesn't have to perfect. Sometimes it is okay to not have everything go according to plans. Sometimes it is okay that all things aren't put back where they belong. It's not easy, but I have to remember that my life isn't about what happens here. I'm trying to make it to Heaven and take as many people as possible with me.

Another thing that made the difference, and this probably was the most difficult, was removing myself from the environment and people that were in my old lifestyle. I know it is easy to say that you have nowhere else to go, or no one else to rely on. But, God is faithful and if you make a determined move He will provide a way of escape. For me it was leaving everything that was mine to sleep in my car until he moved on my Granny's heart to give me a place to stay. It took throwing out my cell phone so I didn't have anyone's phone number from that life. For you it may not take that much, or it may take more, but I truly believe God can and will help you if you are sincere and willing to put in the hard work.

Another lady asked me how I lived with the guilt of what I had done. This is a hard thing. It is something I still battle today. The enemy loves to fight us in our minds. There are always consequences to every choice we make. Loosing those years with my kids is a consequence and I can't get them back. I am always aware of who and what I used to be. One thing I know, and that is even in my darkest days as a Christian I have a peace and hope in God that cannot compare to the sorrow and hopelessness I felt on my best day before I knew Him. "For a day in thy courts is better than a thousand. I had rather be a doorkeeper in the house of my God, than to dwell in the tents of wickedness." (Psalms 84:10). You can take comfort in the fact that there is something bigger than you, every battle you fight, and any enemy you may face, on your side. He loves you simply because you belong to Him. For me it's the same solution. I live on purpose every day. I am determined to be the best I can be at whatever I am doing. I want to be a valuable member of my church, my family, my community, my workplace, and my life. I want people to see me for what God has done in me and not for what my past says I should be. That doesn't mean you will wake up tomorrow and not still be locked up or facing whatever your dealing with in life. But, it does mean that you can go through it with your head high, knowing that you are doing your part and God is taking care of the rest.

Then I challenged them to try it. Get up tomorrow and pray, read the Bible, and then find a way to be better. Maybe, it is being nice to someone you really don't like. Maybe, it is listening to someone or inviting the new lady to sit with you. Maybe, it's calling that person who has hurt you and saying I forgive you because God has forgiven me. When I looked around the room there wasn't a dry eye in the place. I looked over and even the guard in the next room was crying tears of hope and joy. As a side note, some of the guards were open and receptive to us, but some were hard and all business. This guard was all business, and the last person I would even consider having a heart open to God. The next time I came to teach I heard some wonderful testimonies of how the ladies were living on purpose and helping each other overcome. When we share how God has taught, shaped, and given us hope it can move people to receive His word. God can use what he has done in you to inspire and encourage those you share it with.

A group of church friends with a passion for ministry invited me to join them as they evangelized on the streets of our community. I loved the homeless and jail ministry and soon fell in love with street ministry. There were so many amazing things that happened in the streets. God showed up and showed out. We saw many baptized, filled with the Holy Spirit, healed, demons cast out, bellies filled, and hope restored. "And he said unto them, go ye into all the world, and preach the gospel to every creature. He that believeth and is baptized shall be saved; but he that believeth not shall be damned. And these signs shall follow them that believe; in my name shall they cast out devils; they shall speak with new tongues; they shall take up serpents; and if they drink any deadly thing, it shall not hurt them; they shall lay hands on the sick, and they shall recover." (Mark 16:15-18). I learned so much about people. God opened doors that were seemingly closed and padlocked. He used some of the most unlikely people to be His mouthpiece in the street ministry; myself included. There were times people would come to me looking for answers; strangers would walk up to me and say they felt compelled to speak to me for some reason. I had never seen God move so boldly as He did in this season of my life. One Saturday we invited a friend to join us. That Saturday we were visiting a poverty-stricken trailer park in the area, and came across the home of a single mother of ten. The woman's oldest daughter lived there also and had a child. With so many in one home their need was very great. No one in our group had a lot of money, but we put what we had together and went to buy some food for the lady, and all the children. Our friend felt compelled to offer the lady twenty dollars as we got ready to leave. The woman immediately began to cry and let us know that her son had to pay for a trip at school and she had just told him that he couldn't go because she didn't have enough money. The fee was twenty dollars. We saw miracles like these almost every Saturday, but our friend had never experienced anything like this before. He was sharing his experience at the barber shop the following week, and a man that was a manager at a local organic grocery store told him to set up a meeting with our team. We went out to meet this man and were offered to pick up donated groceries a few times a week to provide for the needs of the community. God is so wonderful! This food helped many families who didn't know where their next meal was coming from. For several years the team bought Christmas gifts for needy families, cleaned dirty houses, and visited the lonely. The encounters I saw on the streets were directly from God and I am so thankful to have had those experiences. "Verily, verily, I say unto you, He that believeth on me, the works that I do shall he do also; and greater works than these shall he do; because I go unto my Father." (John 14:12).

Another crossroad in my life was my trip to Peru. My friend and I would visit Lima and few surrounding cities for three weeks. The people were so friendly and wonderful. I love Peru. It will always have a place in my heart. We prayed and fasted for several months prior to the trip. One Saturday, a few weeks before our trip, my friend and I visited a trailer park and had a special encounter with the Lord. The ladies we met received the food and prayer we offered them, but God also had a gift for us that day. During prayer one of the ladies we were visiting prophesied that all that my friend and I would touch would be blessed. She went on to say that God would protect and provide for us wherever our feet would carry us. This lady had no idea about our upcoming travels. On the second night of our trip a new-found friend took us to visit the beach. After sightseeing for a bit we went to sit on the sand and watch the waves come in. We began to share our testimonies with this person. After listening intently for a moment, he asked a question that every Christian soul-winner wants to hear, "What should I do?" I explained Acts 2:38 to him. Letting him know that he needed to repent for all his sins, and explaining that repentance means being sorry, but also turning away from those sins and being determined not to do them anymore. I told him that he needed to be baptized in Jesus name and he would receive the gift of the Holy Spirit as the Bible promises. My friend and I let him know that this is the only way the Bible tells us to be saved. "Jesus answered, verily, verily, I say unto thee, except a man be born of water and of the Spirit, he cannot enter into the kingdom of God." (John 3:5). Our friend

agreed that he needed to be baptized and asked if he could learn

more about living a Christian life. We met many people who were

hungry to know the Lord. God was with us while we were there.

After meeting several people who wanted to be baptized we

connected with a local church and scheduled a time take a group

up to the river for a baptism service. When we first entered that

church, the entire congregation was so excited to see us. They said

that they had been praying and fasting for direction and

breakthrough in ministry, and many had felt that a word would

come from America. When we came in and shared our desire to

have the people we had already met baptized, along with any

others we would meet, they felt this was confirmation. They were

so lovely. They asked us to share our testimonies in the service that

afternoon and the ladies cooked a delicious lunch for us after

service. Unlike many American churches, the congregations in that

area don't have ready access to baptismal tanks. We had plans to

rent two buses to go to the river. We had tracts printed up in

Spanish to pass out in the streets. While visiting the church we asked if anyone would like to go with us to pass out the gospel message and invite people to church. The ladies of that church were so surprised that two women were doing work on the street. This task was one usually only done by men. The men agreed to let their women go out with us and those ladies were thrilled. They were so excited that they met us at the airport on the day we were leaving to say that they were starting a street ministry team. They brought us gifts and said they would never forget how the Lord had opened this door for them. We were so excited the day of the baptism service. We had seen the Lord do so many wonderful things already. We had two buses loaded down with people. It was standing room only. We had bought food, that the ladies from the church graciously prepared for a picnic later that afternoon. I saw God in a different perspective from this country and I was forever changed.

There have been so many times over the years that random people have come up to me at church and slipped money into my hands. They always say the Lord directed them to give. As a single mother there were times these gifts fed us or put gas in our car when I had no way to do either. I am always amazed at God's ability to answer prayers. He answers the ones you ask for and the ones you don't even know to ask for. I have learned this is a Biblical principle. "And it shall come to pass, if thou shalt hearken diligently unto the voice of the Lord thy God, to observe and do all his commandments which I command thee this day, that the Lord thy God will set thee high above all nations of the Earth: and all these blessings shall come on thee, and overtake thee, if thou shalt hearken unto the voice of the Lord thy God." (Deuteronomy 28:1-2).

One Saturday a new man showed up to the church to help with the homeless ministry. My roommate at the time, had met him at a Bible study earlier that week, and invited him to carpool with us. She began telling this man a little about my testimony as we stopped for gas, and when we resumed our trip to Atlanta he shared his with us. I thought the man had an amazing testimony and seemed to be very kind. During our homeless service that day I learned he was also a very passionate worshiper.

On the way back to our cars my roommate mentioned to him that we would be going out in a few hours for street ministry. He seemed interested, so I invited him to join us. He was thankful for the invitation and gladly accepted. Many times, on Saturday, I would come from the homeless ministry and go straight to the prayer rooms at the church to pray for our upcoming street ministry until time to leave. As I went into the prayer room he asked me if he could bring me back some breakfast. I thought that was very nice, but declined. A few weeks later this same man messaged me on Facebook, after a few attempts to contact some of the male group members had went unanswered, to ask how street ministry had went that day. Turns out he was a truck driver and couldn't be in town. We talked through messenger, then text message, and eventually moved to phone calls. I had settled in my mind that I was finished with men. I was happy with the Lord and my ministry. I wasn't looking for a relationship with anyone. This truth is something I shared with my new friend early in our talks. He was the opposite. He wanted a wife and a family. I had wished him blessings with that, and we were happily friends in ministry.

But, there was just some connection neither of us could shake. I wish I could say that we did everything perfectly, but we did not. One thing we knew, and that was that God had put us together. After a very short courtship we were married. Yes, husband number four. I am thankful that God saw our hearts and has blessed our family, even though we didn't follow all the advice we were given, and married rather quickly. I had heard the story of the woman at the well from the Bible. She had issues with men, and many of them, but Jesus went out of his way to visit and save her so that she could in turn be a witness that her town might be saved. "The woman then left her water pot, and went her way into the city, and saith unto the men, Come, see a man, which told me all things that ever I did: is not this the Christ?" (John 4:28-29) I can't compare with any Bible character, but one thing I knew, and that was this time was different. My husband and I love the Lord, we are both in relationship with Him first, and neither of us were looking back. "And if it seem evil unto you to serve the Lord, choose you this day whom ye will serve; whether the gods which your fathers served that were on the other side of the flood, or the gods of the Amorites, in whose land ye dwell: but as for me and my house, we will serve the Lord." (Joshua 24:15).

As with all things in life; the season of street ministry came to an end. Turns out this was perfect timing for my stepdaughter who came to live with us a few months after we were married. I felt lost without my beloved street ministry, but used the spare time to love on my new daughter and my baby boy. I tried to be a good example and mother to them. I tried to teach her to be a woman of the Lord, as her own story of conversion was being written in the pages of time. As both kids headed toward high school graduation our family unit was being molded and shaped. Both young people are remarkable. They have such a passion and desire to work for the Lord. My husband and I are so fortunate to be able to support their ministries as the Lord allows. My husband's youngest daughter, only a little over a year old at the time, also started coming to visit us. I hadn't been mommy to a baby in quite some time. She is a precious child who keeps us all on our toes. How could someone like me deserve these great blessings? This man was so patient and kind with me. I had never been with a man who truly owned his role as head and provider of the home. I am so thankful and blessed for my husband, my boys, and my daughters.

During all my blessings I could feel a darkness starting to creep over me. This darkness was familiar, but I hadn't felt it in a long time. That old enemy of mine, whose name was Depression, was trying to creep back into my life. Isn't that just like the devil? When God is blessing, he looks for ways to slink around and make you question who and what you are. I loved and embraced the avenues of ministry the Lord was allowing me to work in, but, somehow, I felt incomplete. I was still participating in the homeless and jail ministries, but I didn't feel I was doing enough. I had a nagging feeling that something was wrong even though I was the happiest I had ever been in my life.

Like most Christians, I did not ask for prayer from my church family. So many times, we hear preachers reach out to saints of God, and implore them to come to the altar for renewal, but we linger back. We know we need prayer, but we, me, myself, and I stand still writhing in internal anguish unwilling to lose face in front of our fellow church members. That was me at this point. I so desperately needed a break through, but couldn't risk people around me, who loved and cared for my soul, knowing that I might need spiritual assistance. I often wondered if I would ever be able to get back into the place of ministry in prayer that I had once enjoyed with the Lord. I clung to a verse in the Bible that promises we won't lose what the Lord gives us. "For the gifts and calling of God are without repentance." (Romans 11:29). Around this time some dear friends of mine invited me to join a small study on prayer they were having at the church. The meeting was being taught be the same precious elder who years before had encouraged me to pursue becoming a teacher at the jail ministry. This woman is a powerhouse for God and I was honored to hear anything she had to say.

We started with a session on prayer taught by Rev. Mangun "Praying the Tabernacle" (Pentecostals of Alexandria, UPCI). It was remarkable to see how God, in his infinite wisdom, gave us a pattern of prayer way back in the Old Testament days. I learned how to touch the throne of God in these prayer lessons. These were powerful and insightful meetings. I learned so much about prayer and reaching the Lord. I decided one day to put into practice what I was being taught and shut myself in our office room at home. I got on my knees determined not to get up until the dark cloud of depression was lifted from me. I didn't want to be fearful, bitter, or feel inadequate in myself or my walk with God anymore. "But ye, beloved, building up yourselves on your most holy faith, praying in the Holy Ghost, keep yourselves in the love of God, looking for the mercy of our Lord Jesus Christ unto eternal life." (Jude 1:20-21). I had never approached depression in this manner. About ten or fifteen minutes into the prayer I started hearing voices saying that I was being ridiculous and getting nowhere; so, I knew I was on the right path. As I pressed into prayer I could feel the cloud being removed from off me. I couldn't believe it. I had learned to pray and intercede not only for others, but could claim victory in my own situation. I felt a million pounds lighter. The struggles and concerns I had carried for the last several months seemed to vanish. I knew that even though I was no longer in the season of street evangelism in my life the Lord had opened different doors for me.

Miraculously, during these prayer meetings, I also received a word from the Lord regarding my immediate future. My husband and I had often spoke of traveling together, and doing ministry as he drives his semi-truck across the country. As our two middle kids got closer to graduation and heading off to college that dream started to take shape. My husband left his current position to open his own trucking company and pursue his business goals. I was in the best place in my career that I had been in my life. I was making more money than I had ever made. I had recently been promoted and was doing exceptionally well in my new role. But God, knowing what was to come, seemed to put the messages of acting for the Lord, answering His call, and complete trust in His plan on the hearts of so many sermons we were hearing in this exact moment. We prayed and fasted, and I wish I could say we acted without fear, but that wouldn't be true, I left my job to work full time in our new family business. "And he said to them all, if any man will come after me, let him deny himself, and take up his cross daily, and follow me. For whosoever will save his life shall lose it: but whosoever will lose his life for my sake, the same shall save it. For what is a man advantaged, if he gain the whole world, and lose himself, or be cast away?" (Luke 9:23-25). I had spent many years as a single and struggling mother. I had also, with the help of the Lord, worked a job most of my adult life. The thought of walking away from my career and completely trusting my husband to take care of me and our kids was more than terrifying. I was in my fourth marriage and the enemy was trying to tell me that I was putting way too much trust in this relationship. "Commit thy ways unto the Lord; trust also in him; and he shall bring it to pass." (Psalms 37:5). But, I knew my trust wasn't in a relationship; it was in the God who was calling us to a deeper place. "As for God, his way is perfect; the word of the Lord is tried: he is a buckler to all them that trust in him." (2 Samuel 22:31).

I truly believe the Lord gave us a word and a calling and I want more than anything to trust Him with my life. For our entire marriage up to this point my husband had spent most of his time on the road with me and the kids at home. For us to go from that life, to seeing and living with each other every day in the cab of a semi-truck, truly took the help of the Lord. It took us both a lot of time to get over ourselves. There was nowhere to run from each other. To say we had to rely and call upon the Lord in the first few months was an understatement. We both questioned the decision countless times and desired to give up often.

A few weeks into our adventure I was really feeling that it was all a mistake. My husband felt the same way even if he didn't express it verbally. About three am one morning we stopped at a truck stop in the middle of nowhere. As I was standing at the counter, with our coffee, waiting for my husband to finish fueling up the clerk noticed our company name. Apostolic, she remarked, and began to be visibly shaken. I told her that we were Apostolic and that I was traveling with my husband over the road. She began to let me know how she had grown up in the church, but had walked away years ago. She spoke about how her teenage boys were giving her such a hard time and were making all the wrong choices in life. She directly correlated their bad behavior to her decision to leave the church. I began to relay some of my testimony to her, and when my husband came in we asked if we could pray with her. Right there, in the truck stop, in the early morning hours she felt the presence of God for the first time in ages. We encouraged her to find a local congregation to draw strength from and to get back into her Bible. That would be the first of many encounters that would follow in the months to come. I have heard many preachers over the years teach on the call of God. He will call, and then the circumstances will seem impossible, and then He will begin to work in way that you would not have been able to. Accepting the call was easier than waiting on fulfillment.

God had spoken to us about a specific and unique ministry. There are over three million truck drivers in the U.S. If we could reach ten people a day with the gospel message it would take years to reach them all. These men and women, for the most part, spend their time on the road and away from home. They spend even more time alone in their vehicles with brief interactions during stops. It is a population always on the go. We used to say in the street ministry that we would have to revisit some communities every six months or so because their residents were so fluid. But, there is no comparison to the life of a truck driver. I am also learning that beyond the truck there are so many other entities associated with the profession, that there are countless other souls to be witnessed to. We had no idea what this ministry could even look like, how it would operate, or what to do first. And honestly, after a little over a year on the road we are still trusting God to lead us where He wants us to go. We also had to, first and foremost, work and grow the business while on the road. I wish I could report that countless souls have been lead to repentance and saved due to our efforts, but sadly, as with many start up ministries, we know these things take time.

We have made some amazing connections with people all over the country and in Canada over the past year. We have had the opportunity to witness, pray with, and encourage people from coast to coast. We understand that in this ministry we may not see the fruits of our labor. "So then neither is he that planteth anything, neither he that watereth; but God that giveth the increase. Now he that planteth and he that watereth are one: and every man shall receive his own reward according to his own labor. For we are labourers together with God: ye are God's husbandry, ye are God's building. According to the grace of God which is given unto me, as a wise master builder, I have laid the foundation, and another buildeth thereon. But let every man take heed how he buildeth thereupon." (1 Corinthians 3:7-10). On one occasion we were staying at a hotel during a layover. It was during the day time when we arrived, and I noticed the pool was empty so I took the opportunity to go for a swim while my husband rested in the room. I was only out there about ten or fifteen minutes when a lady about my age came to the pool. I could tell by her appearance, and my previous history, that she at some point in her life had issues with drugs. She looked as though she had lived a very rough life. I spoke to her and she said hello and got ready to jump in. I was making small talk, not really thinking that this could be a God moment. Usually, when they occur we aren't really expecting them. Though, the way we live our lives prepares us for just such encounters. "And that he died for all, that they which live should not henceforth live unto themselves, but unto him which died for them, and rose again." (2 Corinthians 5:15). She came right up to me. The woman had no concept of personal space, and she immediately started relaying the tragic events of her life's story. She stated repeatedly that she didn't know why she was telling all of this to me. I could feel the Spirit rising within me and began to share my testimony with her. I told her of the saving and restoring power of Jesus. We spoke for about thirty minutes or so like we were the only people in the world. There was no concept of time or where we were. Soon her fiancé came to join her, and she went on and on telling him about how similar our stories were and how good God is. I went and got my husband, and the couple allowed us to pray with them there at the side of the pool. We all felt the presence of the Lord.

That winter as we were driving through an ice storm, barely able to see the front of the truck, a man called out to my husband over the CB radio, "Hey Apostolic". Our truck has our company name and an image from our favorite witnessing tract, the ACTS 2:38 tract, on the side of the truck. We have gotten several comments about it on our travels. Some are curious about the meaning of the name Apostolic, while others are reminded of tough decisions they have made in their own lives to remove themselves from the faith. My husband answers back and begins a conversation with the man. He said just seeing the name on the side of the truck reminded him about growing up in an Apostolic Pentecostal church. The man had long ago walked away from truth, but his daughters were actively involved in church. There over the mic my husband encouraged and prayed for this backslidden man, who said he knew it was God that engineered the crossing of our paths that day.

There have also been failures and learning curves. One night we stopped at a truck stop and I failed miserably. As I came out of the restroom and wondered around the store waiting for my husband I heard an employee complaining to her coworker. She was going on and on about how miserable the job was, and how badly her life was going. Immediately, I felt a prompting from the Lord to go over to the woman and ask her if I could pray for her. I started to walk towards her and was instantly hit with fear and self-doubt. It seemed so strange to me after having spent so much time in street ministry, and other avenues of ministry, to feel so petrified. I had walked up to strangers on many occasions and shared the gospel. Why was this happening? I continued to make my way to the lady, but stopped just shy of reaching her pretending to look for something on the shelf. The Holy Spirit inside me was screaming for action while every fiber of my flesh was telling me I couldn't do it. My husband came out of the bathroom and I followed him to the truck without saying a word to the woman. I felt wretched. I knew that if I told him what I was feeling he would turn around and make sure we went back to pray for the lady, so I said nothing to him. In the darkness of the truck I cried bitter tears and begged the Lord to send someone more capable to the woman. How terrifying to think that someone's God moment was put into your hands and you dropped the ball. I was a miserable wreck after that. Of course, every ounce of self-worth and belief in my God calling was shaken. I really began to question everything I thought I had heard from the Lord regarding being in the truck. All I could do was repent and ask God to strengthen me and help me to overcome fear. Every time I feel a prompting to speak to someone I remember this situation and the agony of defeat. "If thou, Lord, shouldest mark iniquities, O Lord, who shall stand? But there is forgiveness with thee, that thou mayest be feared." (Psalms 130:3-4).

Through our ministry Facebook page, we try to keep a record of the most notable of our victories for the Lord, and the churches we visit to encourage fellow drivers. We continue to pray often that the Lord will show us how He would have us to go about reaching the truck driving community, while continuing to be a blessing to our family, friends, and local church. I don't know why He chose us, but I know that I can trust him and follow the leading and prompting of his Spirit as we continue our unique path in this specific season.

Just when everything was seemingly perfect in my life tragedy struck. I had spent every Tuesday night for years Granny-sitting. My mom, aunts, and I took turns taking care of Granny. Wheelchair bound and slowly declining in health she became less and less able to take care of her everyday needs on her own. I had spent several years, while I was single, taking care of her much of the time, but as a newly married woman I had to focus my attention on my home. I loved my Granny and still tried to spend as much time as possible with her. Those Tuesday nights were so wonderful. Many times, my boys and step daughter, and later my daughter-in-law and grandkids would join us; we made Tuesday family dinner night. We would cook, eat, and laugh with Granny until her bedtime. When my husband found himself at home on a Tuesday evening he would join us on our Granny family night. The decision to go on the road was so much harder due to having to cut off my Tuesday night visits. I knew I would still see Granny as much as possible when I was home, but it wouldn't be the same. It turns out, as he always does, God was looking out for me. What happened in the next few months wouldn't have been bearable without the physical distance the Lord had allowed between Granny and me. I missed her, as she missed me, and I almost left the road a few times when I felt guilty about not being around.

One Wednesday, as I was praying at the altar at the close of service, a dear friend of mine came up and spoke a word to me. She had no way of knowing what I was going through. I had spoken to my husband earlier that day about Granny. She had been sick, and my family could have really used my help in caring

for her. He said he would support any decision I felt I needed to
make. This dear Sister told me that I needed to follow God's call
on my life and not worry about Granny. He would take care of her
and I was not to lose focus. Wow, God is amazing. "For God has
not given us the spirit of fear; but of power, and of love, and of a
sound mind." (2 Timothy 1:7). With that word I went back to
trucking and trusted God to take care of my sweet Granny.

She was the matriarch of our family and the glue
that bound us all together. One afternoon spent sipping tea with
Granny and you would be caught up on the lives of every family
member. I was on the road when I heard she was in the hospital. I
said prayers and let everyone know I would be home Friday to pay
her a visit. She was all smiles when I entered the room. We picked
up, as we always did, like we hadn't spent a day apart. She was
having some difficulty breathing, but overall seemed to be in good
spirits. We talked for a long while about her being relocated to a
rehabilitation center for further recovery. I just gave praise to God
because she was going to the very facility that our church's
Nursing Home ministry visited every Saturday. After a good long

visit I left to let her rest, and promised to see her at the center the next day for service. When we arrived, I went straight to her room, but she had endured a long night and was still struggling to breath, so she wasn't able to make the service. My wonderful church family, after their service ended, all made their way down to Granny's room, and she had her own personal service. We sang all her favorite hymns, prayed, and spoke words of love and encouragement to her. You could feel the sweet presence of God in that room. "Rejoice in the Lord alway: and again, I say rejoice. Let your moderation be known unto all men. The Lord is at hand. Be careful for nothing; but in everything by prayer and supplication with thanksgiving let your request be made known unto God. And the peace of God, which passeth all understanding, shall keep your hearts and minds through Christ Jesus." (Philippians 4:4-7). I am so grateful for all who took their time to have that special moment with her. I said my goodbyes and let her know I would visit after church the following day. If I had known that would be my last conversation with her I wonder what I would have said differently?

My cousin came to sit with her for the rest of the afternoon and called a short time later to say that her breathing had gotten worse and she was being admitted back into the hospital. By the time we got there they had already incubated her and informed us that we should call the family. I couldn't believe it. I felt as if I were having an out of body experience. I was there, but so over emotional that I just became numb. We were all riddled with grief. There were several who stayed from that day until the end, myself included, it was a vigil we could not be pulled away from. The kids came home from college to be there as they pulled her from life support and sent us over to hospice to wait for the end to come. My lovely daughter took my phone and fielded calls that I was unable to handle from concerned family, friends, and church members. The staff was so patient and kind to us as family members flowed in and out and kept constant watch over her. I was there beside her, as my exhausted family members slept all around the bed, praying that God would give her soul rest and she would have peace. It was so hard to watch her lay there and suffer. I watched as the breath of life left her body. I thanked God for His mercy and for all the years

He had allowed me to have this wonderful lady in my life. I informed the nurse and woke up my family with the news. My husband was a rock for us all. He was so attentive to everyone's needs and I am so thankful for him. During our days at hospice we were able to spread the comfort and peace of God with mourning family members looking for hope. They sat and listened as we sang and praised the Lord, and read the Bible to Granny. They asked questions and sought comfort in the Lord. "I will not leave your comfortless: I will come to you." (John 14:18). God is so good to reach His hand out to those in need. Laying my Granny to rest was one of the hardest things I have encountered. It was a tragedy for us all. Almost a year later I still find myself wanting to call her or tearing up at a memory or place that I shared with her.

# 7 TOO BLESSED TO STRESS

*"Having therefore these promises, dearly beloved, let us cleanse ourselves from all filthiness of the flesh and spirit, perfecting holiness in the fear of God." (II Corinthians 7:1)*

What could a former drug addict, who has had multiple marriages, and is always battling self-esteem issues possibly have to say that the world would be interested in hearing? This is the question that has plagued me for years and hindered my ability to write every word you have read so far. Of course, I know so many others who have lived for the Lord longer than I, and there are those who have known Him on a level I may never reach, and there are sadly so many who survived childhoods far worse than mine, but that doesn't make God any less real to me. "But we have this treasure in earthen vessels, that the excellency of the power may be of God, and not of us." (2 Corinthians 4:7).

I always love to hear the testimony of those who grew up in church. I think theirs are some of the greatest stories being told. What an amazing life to have grown up in grace. Always in the presence of the Lord. Every person at some point will have their own personal encounter with God. There is that moment that He becomes real and personal to you. God doesn't have grandchildren, and expects us all to feel after Him for ourselves. But, hearing the testimony of those standing with him from generation to generation encourages me. I know that the decisions I make today could one day lead to a future generation, from my bloodline, standing to tell an age-old story of trusting in and living for the Lord. The hope in that is just one more reason to march on. "Now the God of hope fill you with all joy and peace in believing, that ye may abound in hope, through the power of the Holy Ghost. And I myself also am persuaded of you, my brethren, that ye also are full of goodness, filled with all knowledge, able also to admonish one another." (Romans 15:13-14).

So, why is what I have to say of any importance? It isn't. I am just one of millions of others who have come to know the Lord. The truth and importance of any testimony is not in the person, or life of the person telling it, but in the Lord, who has provided it. A testimony is something God gives all of us as a tool to reach people and lead them to Him. They are all unique and unable to be argued against. People can debate, pick apart, and twist the Bible, but they can't negate what God has done for you. Your story has happened to you and it is unquestionable to those who hear it. They can't discount how you felt or what you experienced. They can choose to accept and believe it or not, but what we feel and go through in this life belong to us.

I am not a Bible scholar. I know what I read, what I have been taught, and a truth that goes even deeper than that. I know what I have felt through the Holy Spirit that lives within me. I have seen God literally confirm doubts, answer questions, and encourage my sorrowful soul, simply by reading His word. I know that He saved me from myself. When I could find no hope in this world, and had no inner strength to continue to put one foot in front of another, He gave me hope to press on. If it is all a lie and there is no Heaven or Hell; I haven't given up or lost a thing living my life as I do for the Lord. "If in this life only we have hope in Christ, we are of all men most miserable. But now is Christ risen from the dead and become the first fruits of them that slept. For since by man came death, by man also came the resurrection of the dead. For as in Adam all die, even so in Christ shall all be made alive." (1 Corinthians 15:19-22). I have been happy, blessed, comforted, and lifted high above any circumstance life throws my way. My life has been altar'd! But, if it is true and Heaven is real, I am so thankful He lead me to a place where I have been saved in the only way the Bible tells us to be and will one day call it my home. "For he looked for a city which hath foundations, whose builder and maker is God." (Hebrews 11:10).

For a Christian few things are less satisfying than seeing someone else come to the realization that God is real and truly cares for them. I have seen so many eyes light up with that revelation over the years. It is like a switch comes on and they suddenly believe. Once while out with the street ministry team we were giving out food in an apartment complex, as we often did, and we had the opportunity to come into the home of a young lady. When we knocked on the door and told her the reason we were there; because Jesus loved her, and we had a blessing of a few bags of food if she could use it. She immediately began to cry and invited us in. She showed us her cupboards and fridge that were bare. She couldn't afford food, and had children in the home that she didn't know how she would feed. We all shared a personal testimony with her of God's redeeming work in our own lives, and you could see a physical reaction to the good news in her eyes. She wasn't religious, though she believed in God, but she never really considered Him real or relevant to her life. "God shall bless us; and all the ends of the earth shall fear him." (Psalms 67:7). But, that day He came to her front door. I don't know if the lady started living for the Lord, or if she went back to her life after that day, but in that moment, she knew Him to be a real God that loved her. We are called to witnesses but we don't always get to see the fruits of our labors. "Therefore, let no man glory in men. For all things are yours; whether Paul, or Apollos, or Cephas, or the world, or life, or death, or things present, or things to come; all are yours; and ye are Christ's; and Christ is God's." (1 Corinthians 3:21-23). There are so many stories like this that I could relay. God has saved and sent us, as Christians, out into the world with a testimony and a road map; which is His Word to help guide others to Him. "In the beginning was the Word, and the Word was with God, and the Word was God. The same was in the beginning with God. All things were made by him; and without him was not anything made that was made. In him was life; and the life was the light of men." (John 1:1-4). That is our purpose. My life is not about me or what I had to endure but it is about those I have met and have yet to meet. "And he said unto them, go ye into all the world, and preach the gospel to every creature." (Mark 16:15).

I have also learned over the years that ministry happens in so many ways. I make the following points not to brag, but to encourage a deeper sense of involvement and a desire to think outside the box for all those who are reading this book. "Let brotherly love continue. Be not forgetful to entertain strangers: for thereby some have entertained angels unawares." (Hebrews 13:1-2). My husband and I love to entertain at our home. We invite our friends, of course, but we also always look for fringe people to invite. We purposefully search for those not associated with groups in our church and make them feel welcome and loved. These people quickly become a part of our family time and again. We are honored to serve in ministry in our local congregation in a variety of areas. We try, as our schedule permits, to make ourselves available to help in any area that is needed. We have also recently committed ourselves to pre-service prayer. We can't be in every service, but when we are there we try to be at the church early and spend time in prayer for the service, the saints, and lost who will be in God's house that day.

Every ministry in the church is not performed on the platform or in a specialized group. We are all called to ministry if we have been saved. Hosting dinners in your home, even if it is like ours; not the nicest or biggest, and making sure to include someone outside your inner circle is a ministry. My husband is a generous giver. "Give, and it shall be given unto you; good measure, pressed down, and shaken together, and running over, shall men give unto your bosom. For with the same measure that ye mete withal it shall be measured to you again." (Luke 6:38). We are both always looking for ways to bless others in and outside of the church. If we know that members of our church have local business, we try to shop at and support them. Now that we have two kids in Bible college we try to always include, encourage, and bless their friends whenever we visit their respective schools. Being a true friend, an attentive listener, and a valuable church member are also ways to minister. "Bear ye one another's burdens, and so fulfill the law of Christ." (Galatians 6:2). So many times, we, as religious people, believe there is only one type or place of ministry. But, living a dedicated and separated life unto Christ, and following His directions and callings are all apart of ministry. He has gifted us all uniquely and therefore has a unique calling specifically for us. "And it shall come to pass, if thou shalt hearken diligently unto the voice of the Lord they God, to observe and do all his commandments which I command thee this day, that the

Lord thy God will set thee on high above all nations on earth: and all these blessings shall come on thee, and overtake thee, if thou shalt hearken unto the voice of the Lord thy God. Blessed shalt thou be in the city, and blessed shalt thou be in the field. Blessed shall be the fruit of thy body, and the fruit of thy ground, and the fruit of thy cattle, the increase of thy kine, and the flocks of thy sheep. Blessed shall be thy basket and thy store. Blessed shalt thou be when thou comest in, and blessed shalt thou be when thou goest out. The Lord shall cause thine enemies that rise up against thee to be smitten before thy face: they shall come out against thee one way and flee before thee seven ways. The Lord shall command the blessing upon thee in thy storehouses, and in all that thou settest thine hand unto; and he shall bless thee in the land which the Lord thy God giveth thee." (Deuteronomy 28:1-8). What a promise of blessing the Lord has given his people!

I don't know if I will ever completely conquer the battle of the bulge or think that I am good enough. Will I always struggle with my past? I can't take back three failed marriages or the things I did to my children. I don't know what our ministry will look like in a year or ten. Will we see a revival of truck drivers across the nation? Will my husband and I see souls filled with His Spirit and baptized in His name through our efforts? Will we make enough money to continue to bless our children for generations to come and support the work of the church in this world? I don't know, and I can't worry about the answers to those and so many other questions. "In the multitude of words there wanteth not sin: but he that refraineth his lips is wise. The tongue of the just is as choice silver: the heart of the wicked is little worth. The lips of the righteous feed many: but fools die for want of wisdom. The blessing of the Lord, it maketh rich, and he addeth no sorrow to it." (Proverbs 10:19-22).

All I can do is trust God with the life He has given me, and wake up every day with the intention and desire to serve and follow Him. I choose to live my life on purpose for the King of Kings and Lord of Lords despite who or what I am. He saved me for a purpose, His peace truly surpasses our human ability to understand, He is truly an awesome God, and Jesus is His name. "And to make all men see what is the fellowship of the mystery, which from the beginning of the world hath been hid in God, who created all things by Jesus Christ: to the intent that now unto the principalities and powers in heavenly places might be known by the church the manifold wisdom of God, according to the eternal purpose which he purposed in Christ Jesus our Lord: in whom we have boldness and access with confidence by the faith of him. Wherefore I desire that ye faint not at my tribulations for you, which is your glory. For this cause I bow my knees unto the Father of our Lord Jesus Christ, of whom the whole family of heaven and earth is named, that he would grant you, according to the riches of his glory, to be strengthened with might his Spirit in the inner man; that Christ may dwell in your hearts by faith; that ye, being rooted and grounded in love, may be able to comprehend with all saints what is the breadth, and the length, and the depth, and the height; and to know the love of Christ, which passeth knowledge, that ye might be filled with all the fullness of God. Now unto to him that is able to do exceeding abundantly above all that we ask or think, according to the power that worketh in us, unto him be glory in the church by Christ Jesus throughout all the ages, world without end, Amen." (Ephesians 3:9-21).

# ABOUT THE AUTHOR

Crystal Jones is happily married and living a truckers wife life on the road with her husband. They have four children, a daughter in law, and two grandchildren. She has been a regular member of her local UPCI, Apostolic Pentecostal Church, for the past eight years.

This is her debut adventure in writing. She prays that in the telling of her story readers will understand more about His Story and perhaps get a better understanding of how their story can be used to spread the gospel.

The following is one of her favorite portions of scripture.

"Seek ye the Lord while he may be found, call ye upon him while he is near: let the wicked forsake his way, and the unrighteous man his thoughts: and let him return unto the Lord, and he will have mercy upon him; and to our God, for he will abundantly pardon. For my thoughts are not your thoughts, neither are your ways my ways, saith the Lord. For as the heavens are higher than the earth, so are my ways higher than your ways, and my thoughts than your thoughts. For as the rain cometh down, and the snow from heaven, and returneth not thither, but watereth the earth, and maketh it bring forth and bud, that it may give seed to the sower, and bread to the eater: so shall my word be that goeth forth out of my mouth: it shall not return unto me void, but it shall accomplish that which I please, and it shall prosper in the thing whereto I sent it." (Isaiah 55:6-11).

26096979R00076

Made in the USA
Columbia, SC
06 September 2018